The Secrets of Tidepools

THE BRIGHT WORLD OF THE ROCKY SHORELINE

BY VICKI LEÓN

LONDON TOWN PRESS

The London Town *Wild Life* Series
Series Editor
Vicki León

The Secrets of Tidepools
Principal photographer:
Jeff Foott

Additional photographers:
Richard Bucich; Jay Carroll; Forrest Doud; Frederica Georgia;
Richard R. Hansen; George Lepp; Roland and Karen Muschenetz;
Geoffrey Semorile; Stan Thompson; W.E. Townsend, Jr.

London Town Press
P.O. Box 585
Montrose, California 91021
www.LondonTownPress.com

Book design by Christy Hale
10 9 8 7 6 5 4 3 2 1

Printed in Singapore

Distributed by Publishers Group West

Publisher's Cataloging-in-Publication Data
León, Vicki.
The secrets of tidepools : the bright world of the rocky shore-
line / Vicki León ; photographs by Jeff Foott [et al.] —2nd ed.
p. cm. — (London Town wild life series)
Originally published: San Luis Obispo, CA : Blake Books,
©1989.
Summary: Explores the complex ecosystems found in tide
pools, focusing on the life cycles of animals and plants, in text
and full-color photographs.
Includes bibliographic references and index.
ISBN-10 0-9766134-6-8; ISBN-13 978-0976-61346-6
1. Tide pool ecology—Juvenile literature. 2. Tide pools—
Juvenile literature. 3. Tide pool animals—Juvenile literature.
[1. Tide pool ecology. 2. Tide pools. 3. Tide pool animals.]
I. Foott, Jeff. II. Title. III. Series.
QH541.5.S35 L46 2006
577.69—dc22
2006920876

FRONT COVER: At low tide on rocky shores, the sea uncovers its
secrets. Mussels, barnacles, and marine plants grow thickly in
tidepools big and small. Seastars wrestle each other over the
best spots.

TITLE PAGE: The hermit crab uses its huge orange claw to
defend itself and to cut up its food. Dinner is usually a dead or
decaying animal. The hermit eats on the run, shoveling in food
with two sorting paddles near its mouth.

BACK COVER: Tidepool predators hunt in different ways. The bat
seastar pulls prey apart with sticky tube feet. The sea urchin chews
kelp with sharp teeth, while strawberry anemones sting prey
that floats too close. The octopus sneaks up on its dinner targets.

Contents

Spying on a hidden world

▶ The oystercatcher is a regular visitor to the tidepool. This poorly named shorebird seldom eats oysters, preferring to capture limpets and mussels with its sharp bill.

The lowest tides of the year have arrived and I race to get to the beach ahead of the other kids. Shorebirds wheel and cry above me in a tangerine-colored sky. As I run, I catch the cold clean scent of the sea.

What I see isn't the rocky shore I know. Ahead of me stretches a strange land, pitted with silvery mirrors that gleam in the morning light. The mirrors are tidepools, hundreds of them.

My heart races. The sea seldom rolls back its watery blanket this far. There's no time to waste; in a few hours, the sea will hide its secrets again.

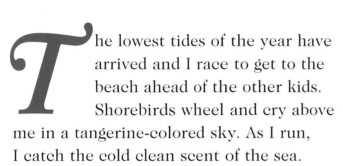

◀ Seabirds and marine mammals like seals and sea otters often live and raise offspring close to tidepools. The tidepool is their convenience store. It's always open, a place where they can snack on crunchy critters and hunt to feed their young.

I head for the water, passing boulders in the splash zone that are freckled with barnacles, periwinkle snails, and chitons. I pass the high tidal zone, where limpets graze and shore crabs scavenge in patches of bright green sea lettuce.

I'm far from the sandy beach now, in the neighborhood my science book calls the intermediate tidal zone. Life is everywhere, crammed into tidepools, flowing out onto stony surfaces. Even the biggest rocks are hidden by the sharp armor of white gooseneck barnacles and blue mussels.

It's hard to find bare rock to walk on, but I do. The slippery algae plants and crowded colonies of snails underfoot may look tough but my teacher says they're as fragile as butterflies.

When I spot two hermit crabs tussling in a tidepool, I stop. One hermit quickly puts the other in a headlock and the little fighters roll over and over, like cartoon figures. The bigger shell thief wins. As I watch, the loser scurries into the other's hand-me-down. I could spend all day with hermit crabs and their nonstop search for the ideal home shell. But other pleasures beckon.

I kneel down, daring myself to touch the flowery petals of a giant green anemone. To me, it feels no rougher than the rasp of a cat's tongue. But its sting can kill a fish. A purple shore crab, one of the tidepool's recyclers, sidles up. It has receptors on its mouth and antennae to track smells—a handy way to find the dead or rotting food it likes. The crab locates a broken sea urchin, then flips the spiny body to nibble the soft underside.

In a look-alike group of aggregating anemones, I notice movement. One of the round squishy creatures begins to stretch like a green rubber band. If only I could linger for hours, I could watch this animal slowly break itself in two, making a perfect clone.

▲ The purple shore crab uses sturdy claws to feed on the dead bodies of fishes and invertebrates. A scavenger, the crab sometimes drops one of its legs to get away from a predator. It can do this without shedding any of its pale blue blood.

►At feeding time, an acorn barnacle among strawberry anemones extends its feathery plumes. Headgear? No—they're legs! Upside-down and unable to see, the barnacle uses its legs to bat food into its body. It may live ten years or more on a diet of floating plankton. After death, its shell stays attached to rocks. Scientists would love to know the secret of the barnacle's super-glue.

But I need to head further out, to the low tidal zone. When I reach my goal, I get on my belly next to a huge tidepool. I try not to move much; even my shadow makes the animals go into hiding.

This tidepool is two feet deep and layered with life. Sponges ooze down rocks, looking like wet throw rugs. Tubeworms build tunnels through patches of juicy-looking strawberry anemones. Surf grass and sleek brown ribbons of feather boa kelp grow thickly.

I gaze into deeper water where the filter feeders are open for business—many of them creatures I've seen only in books. A live scallop shell resembles a half-open smiley mouth as it filters in snowflakes of food. I watch barnacles kicking their feathery legs in rhythm, batting tiny plankton animals into their bodies.

Olive shells and other snails work the bottom of the tidepool, grazing on fuzzy algae that coats everything. Cup corals wave their tentacles, sticky with mucus, to snag floating meals. Blenny fishes snap at the larvae of other fishes.

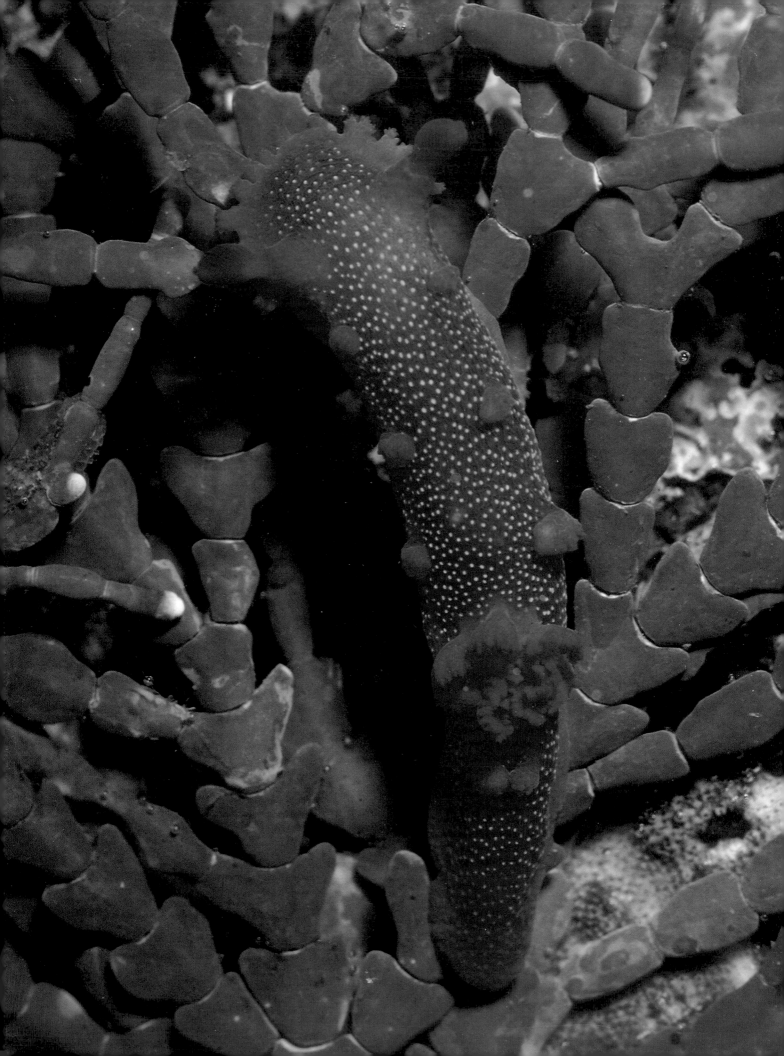

A bat seastar, bright as a tomato, catches my eye. It's found a fat mussel on a rocky ledge and is making a slow-motion attack with its strong tube feet. Once the bat seastar opens a tiny crack in its victim, it will slip its own stomach inside its prey. Then it's goodbye, mussel! as the bat seastar's stomach, a mass of acid and bubbly slime, dissolves the mussel.

I peer into crevices, hoping to spot an octopus or a wolf eel. Instead, I'm startled by a fat sea cucumber that fires its messy innards like a cannonball. My movements must have set off its defensive reflex.

I force myself to sit still again. Soon I get my reward. Suspended from the watery surface of the pool, I spot inch-long nudibranchs, the first ones I've ever seen. These amazing acrobats are snails without shells. Some call them sea slugs, but they're too pretty for that name. One nudibranch wears yellow polka-dots. The other has electric blue feelers and bushy orange spikes. Marine biologists say that the loud colors and patterns of the poisonous nudibranch tell would-be predators, Eat me and you'll be sorry.

The longer I spy on this amazing world, the more awestruck I feel. In my ears, however, the ocean growls ever closer. It's time to retreat to dry land. By now I'm hopelessly hooked on tidepool magic, and I'll be back.

▲ Along California's central coast grows a marine garden. In its beds of bright green sea grass, mixed with algae from brown kelp to rockweed, thousands of tidepool creatures rest, breed, eat, and are eaten.

Ever since that enchanted morning in southern Oregon, I've been a fan of rocky shores and tidepools. These small bright worlds exist along many shorelines on earth. I've explored them in Hawaii and along the coast of New England. I've tidepooled in the Mediterranean waters off Greece and in Mexico's Sea of Cortez. In my home state of California, I've gotten to know countless tidepools.

The Pacific coast, from southern Alaska to parts of South America, is especially rich in these ecosystems. Other tidepool-favored coasts are found around Australia, the British Isles, and the Atlantic north of Cape Cod. Warmer locales with rocky shores and coral formations sometimes have tidepools too.

Tidepools form only in places where rocky shores occur and conditions are right. Marine biologists call this dividing line between land and sea the intertidal zone. I think of tidepools as busy little cities of the sea. They serve as home and nursery, hunting grounds and refuge for hundreds of plant and animal species and millions of individuals.

How do tidepools support such diversity? The first requirement is oxygen—lots of it—supplied by the crashing waves and ocean tides moving in and out. Tidepool plants and animals need lots of nutrients, which are delivered by ocean currents in liquid form and as food particles. Pools with a rich variety of species tend to be found where the weather is temperate or cool and foggy. Rocks with rough surfaces, easy for small creatures to stick to, make the most desirable homes. On the other hand, shorelines that are too hot, too icy, or too sandy are not tidepool-friendly.

Tidepools come in many shapes—not just "pools." They range from tiny basins to large channels, gnawed out of rocks by the teeth of the sea. They occur in sheltered bays and on headlands. Perhaps the most famous is the Great Tidepool of the Monterey peninsula, immortalized by John Steinbeck in his novels.

Why are tidepools constantly revealed, then hidden? As our planet moves in space, it's pulled on by the moon and the sun. That invisible tug-of-war is a force called gravity. At the seashore, we get to see gravity at work on the water itself. Each day and night, the oceans move onto the land of the intertidal and away from it. These regular advances and retreats are called tides.

One of the first secrets I learned as a tidepooler was to make sure I visited them during the lowest tides of the year. These minus tides occur when the earth, moon, and sun are lined up, making the strongest pull of gravity on the ocean waters.

All year long but especially at these times, curious human beings can eavesdrop on a fascinating array of pint-sized wildlife, just as I've done for decades.

◄ Big waves crashing through surge channels bring seawater filled with oxygen and food particles to plants and animals. To live in surge channels, tidepool creatures need to cling very tightly to rocks.

Critters that like a challenge

Intertidal plants and animals are a sturdy bunch that thrive on hardship and extreme conditions. Exposed to air and sunlight for hours, they are later plunged underwater or hit by the sledgehammer of wave action as the tide comes in.

Tidepools tend to be small and shallow, a few inches to a couple of feet deep. During the hours of low tide, seawater evaporates, suddenly making the tidepool more salty. When it rains, the pool loses saltiness. Tidepool residents also get hit with dramatic temperature swings. On hot summer days,

▶Like a city filled with apartments and people, a tidepool is crowded with layers of life. Anemones, algae, sponges, sea squirts, feathery annelid worms, and tunnel-making tubeworms build on top of one another—often for decades. A seastar hunts among them, "running" in slow motion.

▶ The lined chiton grazes on rocks crusted with coralline algae, using the raspy "tongue" on its underside to harvest plants. A day feeder, this inch-long critter often mimics the colors it's found on, letting it hide in plain sight while foraging. Chitons rest in shallow holes they've made in the rock. Sometimes their grip isn't tight enough, and seastars snack on them.

▲ Volcano barnacles get their colors from plant algae growing on them. When exposed to the sun for hours, they keep their sturdy front doors shut. This prevents drying and protects their tender bodies and feeding legs.

an ankle-deep pool can get surprisingly warm.

Most tidepool critters are invertebrates, animals without backbones. Invertebrates may be spineless but they're far from wimpy. To thrive in this challenging environment, they've become tough, ingenious adaptors.

Their biggest challenge? Simply holding on. Tidepool animals and plants have developed diverse ways to cling. Most plants attach themselves to rocks with gnarly fibers called holdfasts. Mussels spin byssal threads to stay put, while barnacles excrete super glues. Seastars rely on hundreds of tubefeet and tidepool fishes have suction cups for traction. Anemones stick themselves in place using gluey mucus on the bottom of their disks.

Sea urchins, limpets, and chitons go about things differently. They grind holes exactly their size out of rock. Urchins make deeper, cavelike holes. The hollows formed by limpets and chitons are used by generations

◄ The opalescent nudibranch, a marine snail without a shell, is smaller than your baby finger. Beautiful and deadly, it attacks anemones, then transfers the unfired stinging cells to the plumes on its own back. The nudibranch also munches hydroids and bryozoans, colonies of tiny animals that look like seaweed.

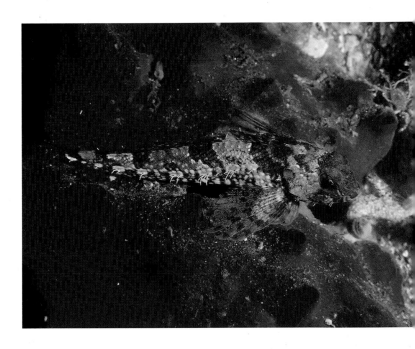

▲ Sometimes called a "tidepool johnny," the sculpin fish hides on sponges and among rocks. It can change color to imitate its background. When the tide comes in, it may venture into another tidepool to eat.

of animals; each creature finds its way back home by following a chemical trail.

To cope with extremes of temperature and dryness, animals adapt in different ways. At low tide, anemones and sea cucumbers change shape, rolling themselves into balls to conserve moisture. Snails tightly close, using their foot as a door. Barnacles store water inside their armored shells, then slam the plates shut.

Some tidepool animals use gills to breathe underwater but have a high tolerance for air. Crabs, for example, roam widely. When they need moisture, they often hide out under wet seaweed.

Almost every creature is the favorite food of another, so blending in is important. Sculpin fishes and octopuses have special chromatophore cells in their skins. With these cells, they can change colors to match backgrounds. Chitons, abalones, and top snails get part of their protective coloration from the foods they eat.

▲ Leaf or gooseneck barnacles wear armored plates to protect their soft bodies. At feeding time, they extend rubbery "necks" that bend with the waves in order to catch nearly invisible floating animals and plants called plankton.

A few animals take the opposite approach. Instead of camouflage, nudibranchs advertise. Most of these poisonous little hunters wear wild colors and bushy gills as dazzling headgear.

In this complex ecosystem, plants and animals share another surprising trait. Many of them grow slowly and for a very long time. Seastars and brown kelp survive up to 20 years; anemones and sponges may grow for centuries. The common mussel takes three years to reach full size. Even a tiny barnacle often lives into its teens.

Over time, the most successful tidepool species have expanded their ranges. Called indicator species, these familiar faces include seastars, mussels, barnacles, anemones, and hermit crabs. Marine biologists further organize these living things according to the part of the intertidal zone in which they live—although some can be found in more than one place.

The splash or spray zone is home to the toughest organisms, at home on land and sea. They tend to be small animals: barnacles, limpets, rock lice, crabs, chitons, and snails like the whelk and periwinkle. A few algae that can take the wet-to-dry environment live here. This zone also receives visitors, such as seagulls and oyster-catcher birds hunting the occasional shore crab.

The high tidal zone stays more moist, its rocks and pools slippery with rockweed, bright green sea lettuce, and other algae. Mussels, turban snails, and gooseneck barnacles make their appearance here.

The floors of the intermediate tidal zone are crowded with aggregating and giant

▼ Like other seastars, bat seastars have no eyes. Instead, they have light sensors at the tips of their arms. It's normal for bat seastars to sport between four and nine arms. These hungry hunters eat plants and animals, living and dead; they keep from being eaten by using a chemical repellent.

►Brittle stars scavenge at night, hiding by day in sparkly heaps under rocks or inside of friendly sponges. They can't take the sun or wave shock, so they live in the lowest intertidal zone. They can't take stress, either. At the first sign of trouble, a brittle star skedaddles, shedding an arm or two. This defensive move is called autotomy.

green anemones, cup corals, grazers like sea urchins and hunters like seastars. Hermit crabs and olive shells scurry about. Marine plants, including one called dead man's fingers, cover the rocks, competing with thick colonies of mussels and barnacles.

In the low tidal zone, uncovered a few times a year, strawberry anemones and other anemones flourish, along with feathery annelid worms, nudibranchs, sponges, sea urchins, sea cucumbers, and sunflower seastars. Coralline sculpins use sucker pads to cling to rocks; at high tide, they surf in to hunt shrimp in pools closer to shore. On the rock walls of the tidepool and in dense sandy beds of seaweed dwell clams, scallops, and oysters.

Under boulders hide brittle stars and burrowing worms. Inside crevices and caves lurk octopuses, eels, and spiny lobsters. Rock surfaces are also covered with lacy bryozoans, colonies of plumelike hydroids and tunicates that look like light bulbs. In this thick glowing carpet of living matter, it's hard to tell which organisms are plants and which are animals, or where one individual ends and another begins.

▲ Like other tidepool fishes, the blue-banded goby has a suction cup on its underside that lets it stick firmly to rocks, avoiding wave damage.

All manner of mealtimes

The average tidepool is swimming in more things to eat than you could find in all the delicatessens in New York City. The pool itself is a rich soup of organic life, constantly refueled by the tides. It's chock full of plankton, from plant matter like diatoms to microscopic animals like copepods and squid larvae. Tidepool soup gets extra flavor from detritus, a word used to describe dirt, dead animals, droppings, molted skin, and other leftovers.

◄ Herring gulls feed on clams, fishes, and weirder food items from garbage to scratchy seastars. They live along the shore where the pickings from tidepools and gullible tourists are good. Adult gulls have four-foot wingspans and hoarse, yodeling cries. Chicks soon learn to peck at the red spot on the lower beak of their parents to get lunch.

Nothing edible is wasted here. Sea hares and other animals regularly vacuum the tidepool floor. Worms and other burrowing creatures eat what looks like bare sand, yet each grain carries a film of nourishment.

Cone-shaped limpets grind across rock surfaces, foraging for algae. Although they seek vegetable matter, limpets sometimes bulldoze away barnacles too young to have gotten a good grip on the rocks.

Limpets, chitons, snails, abalones, and other mollusks do their grazing with the radula, an organ on their undersides that acts like a rough toothy tongue. If we could eavesdrop on the sounds of a tidepool, we would hear them crackling their way across kelp or coralline algae. The champion of crunch? The sea urchin, a spiny fellow that regrows the five sharp teeth on its underside every few months.

Tube snails go fishing to find food, spinning nets of mucus to catch detritus and plankton. Once they've caught their limit, they reel it in, gobbling net and all.

Many tidepool animals glue themselves to rocks and filter feed, letting the restless tides deliver the delicatessen to them. Filter

feeders extend feathery legs, tube-like siphons, or mucus to catch food particles, sometimes slurping them like spaghetti. Barnacles, mussels, sponges, tunicates, and bivalves like oysters and clams eat in this way. So do brittle stars at times.

Members of the anemone family sit where the water flows hardest, waving their graceful tentacles to catch the food washing by them. Some species are able to move to more favorable feeding spots, creeping slow as molasses to get there. Most anemones dine on crabs, mussels, and fishes. The anemone brings dinner to its mouth, then stings it with special barbed cells in its tentacles called nematocysts. After that jolt, most prey is in no shape to escape.

The sea cucumber has sticky tentacles to collect its dinner. After stuffing food into its mouth, the sea cuke licks its tentacles, looking just like a kid eating cookie batter off a spoon.

Scavengers live on dead tissue, mostly animal. Brittle stars, true crabs, lobsters, and small fishes such as sculpins and gobies scavenge most of their meals. So does the hermit crab. It zips around, using its

◄ Moving on long spines and tube feet, the purple sea urchin goes after vegetables, especially kelp. To chew, it has five sharp teeth on its underside. When not kept in check by sea otters, armies of urchins may do great damage to kelp forests offshore.

▼ Orange cup corals are the only hard corals found in Pacific coast tidepools. The cup coral attaches itself to rocks, then builds a stony base to protect its soft polyp body and 36 feeding tentacles.

smaller claws to toss every small morsel it finds in the direction of its piehole. Two paddles near its mouth work nonstop to sort the tasty bits from the inedibles.

Many tidepool dwellers are predators, hunting other animals for a living. Seastars, nudibranchs, Thai snails, and octopuses use hunters' tricks to capture prey: strong sticky tube feet, toxic bites or stings, organs that drill through shells, and camouflage.

The octopus is the smartest invertebrate in the world, not just the tidepool. A master of disguise, it tiptoes up to a fish or floats down on an unsuspecting crab like a parachute of death. Its eight arms are covered with several million receptors, letting it "taste" everything it touches. The soft body of this tidepool Terminator

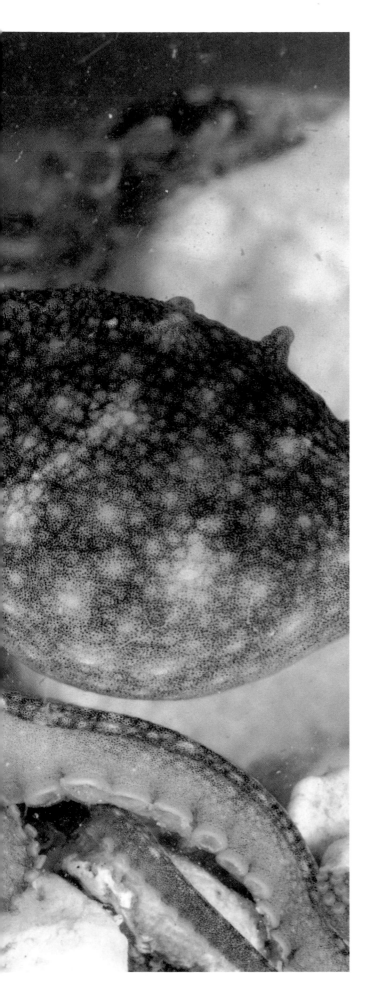

◄ The two-spotted octopus is ten to 30 inches of slippery cephalopod. This shy hunter uses thousands of suckers and keen eyes, located above its blue "eyespots," to capture crabs and fishes. The octopus often changes color and shape to stalk its prey— and hide from enemies. Its fake eyespots help fool predators, too.

conceals a poison-shooting organ to stun prey and a sharp beak to chop it up.

The fingertip-sized nudibranch is just as deadly as the octopus. Although small and soft-bodied, it routinely hunts large scary opponents like jellyfish and anemones. It swallows their stinging cells along with its meal, then stores the unfired weapons in its own body. When two nudibranchs meet, one often devours the other. This tendency toward cannibalism makes nudibranch mating an adventure at times.

Tidepool hunting activities and mealtimes are moveable, depending on the ebb and flow of ocean tides. Some animals hunt as the tide comes in. The seastar, for example, moves from home base toward dry land to feast on mussels, chitons, and snails. It can find, open, dissolve, and eat a 4-inch abalone in a couple of hours—then move back into wetter territory. Light and darkness also determine tidepool activity. Scavengers like brittle stars and grazers like chitons usually feed at night, when risks are less.

Except for surf grass, tidepool plants belong to the huge algae family. Like plants on land, they use sunlight to photo-

►A seastar has no teeth or jaws. Instead, it uses hundreds of strong, sticky tube feet to pull its victim apart—in this case, a black chiton. Once the chiton is in pieces, the seastar ejects its stomach over it. The seastar's acid juices slowly "melt" the chiton, digesting it.

synthesize. They cling with fibers called holdfasts and have no roots to take up nutrients. Instead, wave action brings them a liquid diet. Marine plants form thick curtains, which become important hiding places for animals in this invertebrate-eat-invertebrate world.

▼ Young abalones use tidepools as nurseries, grazing on kelp plants to grow bigger. Pink coralline algae sometimes grows over the ab, a disguise that helps it escape the attention of sea otters and other predators.

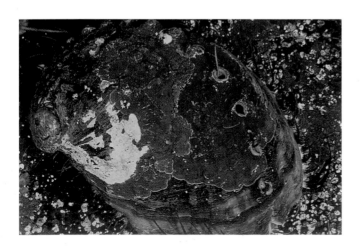

The mating game, played many ways

▶ Sea snails called nudibranchs don't need shells. They are small but fiesty hunters. When two of the same species meet, they sometimes mate. The nudibranchs in this photo are different species, so they may fight. Or eat each other!

When it comes to reproduction, human behavior is pretty ordinary compared to the unusual methods of a nudibranch, an anemone, or even a piece of kelp.

Scientists use two categories to describe how living things multiply: sexual and asexual. Sexual reproduction means that two organisms combine their DNA heritage to form a genetically new individual. Asexual reproduction means that a plant or an animal creates a new but genetically identical organism by splitting or cloning itself.

Within these two categories, tidepool animals and plants reproduce in an astonishing variety of ways.

Take the nudibranch, for instance. This small hunter is a hermaphrodite, meaning that each individual has male and female organs. When the Spanish shawl nudibranch ripples its magenta-and-purple body up to a suitable mate, they simultaneously exchange sperm and fertilize each others' eggs. This doesn't always go well. As they mate, they sometimes bite each other, which can lead to one nudibranch becoming lunch instead of a parent.

These touchy little animals have a complex life cycle. They begin as eggs, then hatch into sea-going larvae that wander far and wide. Larvae that escape being eaten soon change into adult nudibranchs. Crabs, barnacles, abalones, mussels, snails, sea hares, and other tidepool invertebrates also cycle from eggs to larvae to adults.

Worms, chitons, sea urchins, seastars, and other animals reproduce quite differently. They shoot clouds of eggs and sperm into the water, counting on the movement of water to join the two for fertilization. Sometimes groups of these animals will spawn all at once, taking their cues from phases of the moon, sun, and time of year.

The octopus mates by copulating, body to body. So do sculpin fishes and the heavily armored crab. To succeed, crabs must time mating with molting. After the female sheds her shell, the male embraces her, then stands by protectively while her new shell hardens. Only then does the male crab molt, shedding his old carapace for a larger one. Crabs are among the few tidepoolers to make courtship displays. Male crabs dig burrows, then wave their claws to entice females.

►Mating while wearing a hard shell is nearly impossible. To solve the problem, the male crab carries the female until she loses her shell. After they mate, he hangs around to protect her until her new shell hardens and she's no longer defenseless. The female will carry her purple eggs, now fertilized, for eight months.

▲A giant green anemone begins to release white sperm. With luck, it will float through the sea and find a cloud of eggs to fertilize nearby. This is called broadcast spawning. Some anemones can also reproduce asexually. This means they can clone exact copies of themselves.

If you thought nudibranchs were odd, wait until you hear about the private lives of anemones. These animals regularly split themselves in half. Called cloning or fission, this process takes about two days. At other times, anemones reproduce sexually. Males release smoky clouds of sperm which drift in hopeful search of clouds of eggs from female anemones. A few anemone species even give birth to live offspring.

Still other species are hermaphrodites, such as the brooding anemone. This creature creates its own offspring without any help from other anemones. Inside its body, the brooder fertilizes its own eggs. They turn into larvae, which then exit through the anemone's mouth. The youngsters embed themselves at the base of their parent's pedal disk, growing for three months until they're big enough to fend for themselves.

As if that weren't a good enough party trick, the brooding anemone can also

► Flexible sea palm plants bend easily and grow in places where waves hit hard and often. Instead of roots, they grip rocks with huge holdfasts, a mass of rough, tough tendrils.

multiply itself while it's in motion! To get underway, it releases its sticky pedal disk from the tidepool floor, then does a slow-motion somersault. As it moves, the brooding anemone tears off bits of its disk, each bit growing into a new clone of itself. This painful-sounding approach to parenthood is called pedal laceration.

Marine plants also propagate in odd ways. The sea palm, an upright annual, positions itself on rocks where the wildest waves hit. At low tide, it releases millions of seeds called spores onto the exposed rocks. Talk about pressure: the sea palm spores have only a few hours to attach themselves and sprout before the tide comes in.

Many tidepool plants play hide and seek, alternating between sexual and asexual reproduction. The brown fronds of kelp and the green beds of sea lettuce, so visible around tidepools, are the showy phases of plants alternating between the two types of reproduction.

Cooperating & other ways to survive

In the crowded conditions of the tidepool, residents use many strategies to survive, such as autotomy. That word means the ability of animals without backbones to shed limbs or body parts without harm, later regrowing them.

Why do animals voluntarily shed their parts? Sometimes a body part gets trapped between rocks or harmed by wave action. Most of the time, however, autotomy helps animals outsmart predators. A crab about to become the main dish of an octopus finds it very useful to drop its claw and run for it, distracting the octopus with a snack.

Crabs, shrimp, and lobsters, all of them decapods or 10-legged creatures, are

◀ Instead of taking a live seastar from its tidepool home, choose a dried seastar, harvested professionally. Two of the dried seastars in the photo show the marvelous ability of some creatures to shed their arms and then regrow them. This magic feat, called autotomy, is a seastar specialty.

▼ Like other invertebrates, a crab can lose one of its body parts without harm. This escape behavior is called autotomy. In its lifetime, this 10-legged red crab may lose a leg or two and regrow them both.

champs at autotomy. Fan worms and other burrowers can also fling away their brightly colored gills and tentacles when startled.

Who has the weirdest display of autotomy? The sea cucumber. When nettled, this foot-long warty pickle spews out all of its internal organs. This unpretty sight may alarm its attackers as well as give them a messy snack, leaving the sea cuke to regrow its guts at leisure.

The real star of autotomy is, appropriately enough, the seastar. I once found a seastar trapped between rocks, which was busy twisting its body away from the captive arm until it broke off. I later learned that seastars can close off blood vessels to their limbs so they don't bleed to death. Once a flap of membrane seals the wound, a new limb will begin to grow.

Tidepool survival also depends on safety

▼ A sunflower seastar begins adult life with just six rays or arms. As it gets older, it adds arms—up to 20 more. This huge and sticky predator can move up to four feet a minute on its 15,000 tube feet. No wonder that other critters, even spiny urchins, run away from it.

in numbers. Biologists call this strategy aggregation. Brittle stars, anemones, mussels, and other animals tend to grow in groups. Living in clusters seems to give them greater protection against oxygen suffocation and higher resistance to poisons.

Although competition for food and shelter in the tidepool is fierce, it is also balanced by cooperative behavior. Tidepool invertebrates form all kinds of helping alliances. Certain crabs grow their own camouflage by planting and tending gardens on their backs. Some of the "flowers" are tiny animals, like bryozoans. When the crab molts its carapace each year, it carefully replants its garden on its new shell.

Hermit crabs are also generous hosts, sheltering bristleworms and letting slipper snails brood their eggs within their shells. Hermits also decorate their shells with tiny stinging anemones as protective bodyguards. In turn, the anemones feast on the food dropped by this messy eater.

Another partnership has the sculpin fish joining forces with a sea urchin. The wicked armor of the urchin offers protection to the sculpin, who returns the favor by keeping the urchin's spines tidy.

Sponges often share quarters with barnacles. With its active legs, the barnacle catches more food particles, so both filter feeders benefit. The sponge is slippery, which keeps the tube feet of hungry seastars from getting a grip on the barnacle.

The giant green anemone partners with algae that go to work, producing oxygen and sugars for it. Inside the body of the meat-eating host, the algae plants get a safe sunlit bed plus organic compounds they can use.

Not so long ago, scientists had little idea of the diversity and harmony of these partnerships between different species. Now that we've learned about tidepool cooperation, maybe it's time to put it to work in our own human societies.

▼ The tidepool world is a busy recycling center. Today, these turban snails gobble the fronds of a kelp plant. Tomorrow, they will make a meal for a seastar. Next week, their empty shells will become new homes for hermit crabs.

► At low tide, the giant green anemone sags like an old beanbag. When the sea returns, it opens into a flower, its dancing "petals" full of stinging cells that paralyze prey. This species may live for hundreds of years and get as big as a plate; it will even tackle a dogfish shark. The anemone borrows its color from plant algae inside it. The two share resources, another example of tidepool cooperation.

Saving our tidepools

We share the earth and sea with uncounted millions of plants and animals. Most of the time, we cannot share their worlds. Their habitats are too tiny, too nocturnal, too inaccessible. Along rocky shores, however, we're given the opportunity of passing through the looking-glass into the tidepool world. In a single tidepool, we are privileged to see a rich and busy ecosystem in intimate detail.

Strong waves and weather extremes rarely defeat the tidepool creatures. Their homes, however, are easily sickened by runoff or pollution, quickly destroyed by commercial development. Even when we don't mean to, we love wildlife and wild ecosystems to death. All too often, popular tidepools from California to Washington, from Hawaii to Mexico, suffer from overuse, their plants and animals shattered and broken by too many human feet.

As sturdy and successful as these plants and animals are, they have no defenses against careless collectors and uncaring litterbugs.

Please walk lightly out here. Look for bare rocks to step on, and take care not to trample or crush the plants and animals that cover almost every surface. Take photos, not animals or shells. Remember that every living thing you see is protected by law—even things you may not recognize as living. Ripping seastars from the rocks destroys the tube feet they hunt with; even gentle handling dries out tidepool critters and can kill them.

Be patient. Sit tight at one pool, giving the critters a chance to emerge and go about their business. Always keep one eye on the restless ocean while you gaze your

◄ Tidepools on beautiful shorelines from California's Big Sur, pictured here, to New England and Hawaii grow more and more popular. Certain tidepools sometimes get loved to death by human beings, who trample and pollute them, killing their fragile inhabitants.

▲ To preserve the magic of tidepools, visitors need to take photos, not shells or live critters. To preserve themselves, photographers and other curious human beings need to keep an eye on the restless sea as they eavesdrop on tidepool activity.

▲ Brown algae, often called kelp, grows in abundance on rocky shores and around tidepools. One plant may live up to 15 years, providing food and shelter for countless creatures.

fill at this bright world. Before you leave, make sure each tidepool rock, shell, and pebble is returned, right side up, to its place. That way, tidepoolers for generations to come will share the magic you and I have found here.

Tidepool secrets

- Seastars have no eyes but can see light and dark through sensors on the tips of their arms.

- Crabs have pale blue blood and can lose a leg or two without pain or bleeding. Why do they do it? To escape hungry predators.

- The tiny nudibranch has super powers. It eats prey filled with stinging cells, then transfers the deadly weapons into its own soft body for defense.

- Adult barnacles are blind and live upside-down, kicking their feathery legs to collect food morsels that pass by.

- Although they seem glued in place, seastars, anemones, and sea urchins do move—usually at a snail's pace. When a hungry seastar approaches a sea urchin, however, it moves away at three times its normal speed.

- Anemones have many ways to reproduce. Sometimes they shoot clouds of sperm and eggs into the water. At other times, they split in two, making clones or copies.

- Tidepool critters eat in different ways. Sea hares vacuum dirt off the tidepool floor. Mussels use hairs to draw in food particles. Tube snails cast nets made of mucus to fish.

- To protect their soft rear ends, hermit crabs borrow vacant shells to wear, often fighting with each other over shell homes.

- The giant green anemone gets big as a plate. When grown, its stinging cells can even kill a dogfish shark.

▶The hermit crab protects its soft hindquarters by wearing another critter's shell, recycling it for larger ones as it grows. This blue-legged hermit in a Pacific tidepool tries on a turban snail shell decorated with a hitchhiking limpet. In Atlantic tidepools, hermits go after the shells of moon snails and periwinkles.

Glossary

Aggregation. A "safety in numbers" defense strategy used by anemones and other tidepool creatures that live in clusters.

Algae. The simplest forms of plant life, kelps and rockweed are examples of algae species living in salt water.

Asexual reproduction. The ways in which a plant or animal reproduces a genetically identical copy of itself, such as cloning, fission, or pedal laceration. Many tidepool organisms reproduce this way.

Autotomy. The ability of seastars, crabs, and other invertebrates to shed limbs or other body parts, then regrow them. Autotomy is often used to escape predators.

Broadcast spawning. A method of sexual reproduction used by sponges and other tidepool animals. They shoot eggs and sperm into the water at the same time to scatter or broadcast them.

Byssal threads. Strong, hair-like fibers produced by mussels and other mollusks to attach themselves to rock surfaces.

Carapace. The hard shell or exoskeleton of lobsters, crabs, and other crustaceans, shed each year as the animal grows and molts.

Chromatophores. Specialized skin cells that can create rapid color changes; they're found in octopuses and certain fish species.

Copepods. Small shrimplike animals, the most numerous species on earth. They occur in huge swarms in the ocean and are the main food supply for a food web of larger creatures. Krill, also tiny and numerous, are similar to copepods.

Detritus. Tiny particles of organic waste, from rotting meat to dirt; an important food for many tidepool creatures.

Diatom. A common alga, one of many microscopic plants that form part of the "soup" of free-floating plankton in the ocean.

◀ Wrack is the name given to the tangle of plants and animals washed up on rocky shores. Although the green kelp, red Turkish-towel algae, and white coralline algae are no longer alive, their bodies provide food and shelter for beach hoppers, crabs, and other marine creatures.

Hermaphrodite. An organism with male and female sex organs. Many tidepool creatures, including barnacles and nudibranchs, are hermaphrodites.

Holdfast. A mass of tough fibers, used by kelp to cling to rocks. Most marine plants have no roots, depending on holdfasts instead.

Invertebrate. Animals without backbones, the most abundant group of animals in the ocean.

Larva/larvae. The second stage of growth in the young of crabs, anemones, seastars, and others. After hatching from eggs, larvae float or swim in the ocean before changing into their final adult form.

Mantle. The fleshy part of nudibranchs and snails. From the mantle, snails secrete substances that harden to form their own shells.

Molting. An annual stage in the lives of crabs and other marine invertebrates. As they grow, they shed their hard shell or carapace, replacing it with a new one.

Mutualism. The helping behaviors or cooperative living arrangements between tidepool plants and animals, or between one animal species and another.

Nematocysts. Harpoon-like stinging cells located in the bodies of some tidepool predators, such as anemones.

Nudibranchs. Small, often colorful predatory snails without shells, found in tidepools and deeper waters.

Pedal disk. The flat base or foot of an anemone.

Plankton. The rich living "soup" of the sea, made of free-floating plant matter like algae and diatoms, and animal matter like larvae, krill, and copepods. Plankton washes through tidepools and nourishes the entire web of life in the sea.

Radula. The scraping organ on the underside of many tidepool grazers, such as chitons and snails.

Spore. A tiny reproductive body used by some plants; most marine plants reproduce using spores instead of seeds.

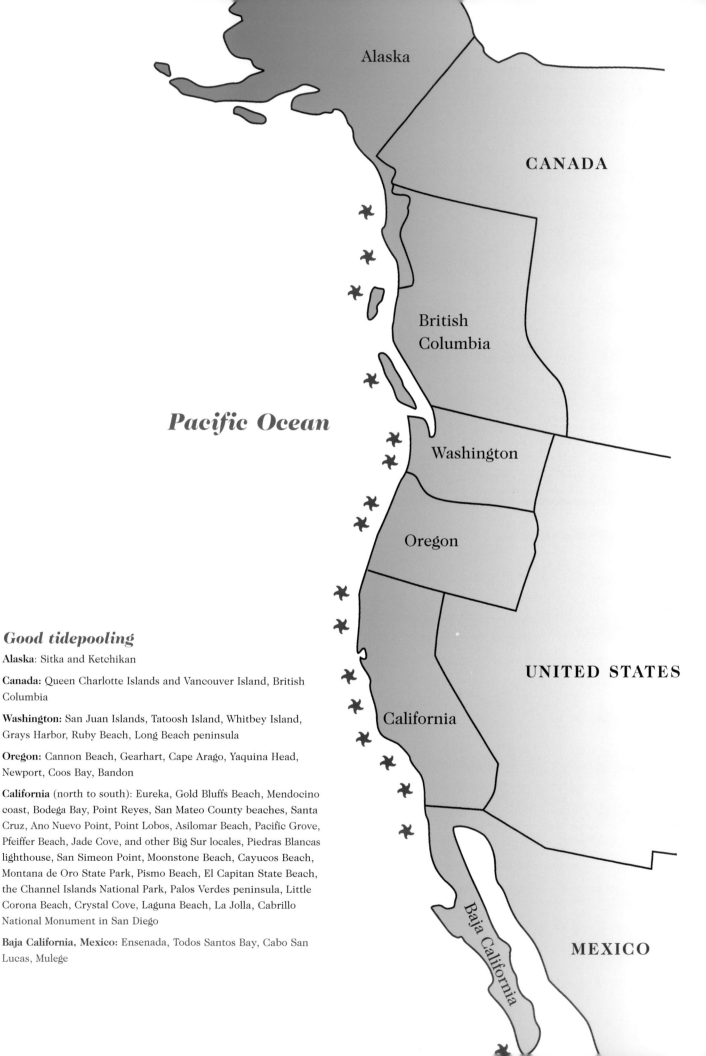

Alaska

CANADA

British
Columbia

Pacific Ocean

Washington

Oregon

UNITED STATES

Good tidepooling

Alaska: Sitka and Ketchikan

Canada: Queen Charlotte Islands and Vancouver Island, British Columbia

Washington: San Juan Islands, Tatoosh Island, Whitbey Island, Grays Harbor, Ruby Beach, Long Beach peninsula

Oregon: Cannon Beach, Gearhart, Cape Arago, Yaquina Head, Newport, Coos Bay, Bandon

California (north to south): Eureka, Gold Bluffs Beach, Mendocino coast, Bodega Bay, Point Reyes, San Mateo County beaches, Santa Cruz, Ano Nuevo Point, Point Lobos, Asilomar Beach, Pacific Grove, Pfeiffer Beach, Jade Cove, and other Big Sur locales, Piedras Blancas lighthouse, San Simeon Point, Moonstone Beach, Cayucos Beach, Montana de Oro State Park, Pismo Beach, El Capitan State Beach, the Channel Islands National Park, Palos Verdes peninsula, Little Corona Beach, Crystal Cove, Laguna Beach, La Jolla, Cabrillo National Monument in San Diego

Baja California, Mexico: Ensenada, Todos Santos Bay, Cabo San Lucas, Mulege

California

Baja California

MEXICO

About the Author

Vicki León is the Series Editor for the London Town Wild Life series. She's also the author of 32 books, including titles for this series on sea otters, seals, and parrots in the wild.

Photographers

Jeff Foott, principal photographer for this book, contributed 19 photos, including seven closeups of tidepool creatures. Ten other wildlife photographers helped capture the flavor of tidepool life: Richard Bucich, pp 19, 28-29, back cover; Jay Carroll, front cover, p. 11; Forrest Doud, p. 33; Jeff Foott, pp 1, 4, 5, 6, 7, 8, 9, 15, 17, 18, 21, 22, 24, 25, 28, 32 left & right, 39, 43; Frederica Georgia, p. 40; Richard R. Hansen, p. 42, top ; George Lepp, pp 26-27, 37; Roland and Karen Muschenetz, pp 10, 14, 16, 36, 38, 42 bottom, 44-45; Geoffrey Semorile, pp 12-13, 31, back cover; Stan Thompson, pp 34-35; W.E. Townsend, Jr, p. 20.

Special thanks

- Diana Barnhart, Education and Marine Science Advisor to the Wild Life series
- Richard R. Hansen, wildlife photographer & biologist

Where to see tidepools

Please be respectful of animals and plants when tidepooling; popular spots are at risk of becoming heavily trashed "dead zones" from too much human traffic.

In the wild: To visit Pacific coast tidepools, please see our "good tidepooling" map on these pages with suggested locales from Alaska south to Baja California, Mexico.

Wild tidepooling elsewhere:
In the Hawaiian Islands: at Kaumalapau on Lanai and at Waiopae on the big island of Hawaii.

Along the Atlantic coast, rich tidepools are found at Acadia National Park and Bar Harbor, Maine, and at the Seacoast Science Center in Rye, New Hampshire

Tidepool displays and exhibits: Many aquaria, zoos, marine centers, and marine sanctuaries offer tidepool displays and hands-on touch pools. Some have artificial tidepools filled with live plants and animals. They include:

- British Columbia: Vancouver Aquarium in Vancouver; Sealand in Victoria
- Washington: Seattle Aquarium; Point Defiance Zoo & Aquarium in Tacoma
- Oregon: Hatfield Marine Science Center and Oregon Coast Aquarium in Newport
- California: Steinhart Aquarium in San Francisco; Monterey Bay Aquarium in Monterey; Channel Islands Visitor Center in Ventura; Cabrillo Museum in San Pedro; Sea World, Cabrillo National Monument, Scripps Aquarium, and the Natural History Museum in San Diego

Helping organizations and good websites

- Monterey Bay Aquarium has touch pools and other hands-on exhibits plus a sparkling website with current information about tidepools and snappy profiles of the creatures in them. Remarkable photos plus "candid" clips of tidepool critters hunting, feeding, and mating. (www.mbayaq.org)
- The National Marine Sanctuaries program has a rich website, with video clips on nudibranchs. Click through to its online guide to responsible tidepooling and marine wildlife watching, a worthwhile download: (www.oceanservice.noaa.gov)
- Earthwatch Institute, 3 Clock Tower Place, #100, Maynard MA 01754. This global organization gets results, linking scientists, teams of volunteers, and research projects on nearshore habitats, sharks, invertebrates, coastal ecology, and much more. Teams in more than 50 countries; some take families, teens, and kids ten and up. Teachers and students: check their website for special deals, scholarships, curriculum materials, and "Live from the Field" opportunities. (www.earthwatch.org)
- Oceanlink is a splendid interactive site where kids from all over the world can "Ask a Scientist" and get answers from experts. Check out their "All about the Ocean" section. (www.oceanlink.island/net/ask)
- The Cabrillo Aquarium has touch tanks and hosts fun events from tidepool walks to grunion runs. (www.cabrilloaq.org/critter1.htm)
- National Geographic offers breaking news on marine biology, tidepool creature features, and more. (www.nationalgeographic.com)

To learn more

Books

- *Intertidal Wilderness.* By Anne Wertheim. (U. California Press 2002) Unusual behavioral photos in tidepools and deeper waters.
- *Oceans* and *Seashore.* By April Sayre (21st Century Books 1997). Great pair of books on watery worlds for 4th to 7th graders.
- *A Living Bay: the Underwater World of Monterey Bay.* By Libby and Lowell Langstroth. (U. California Press and Monterey Bay Aquarium 2000). More than tidepools; totally fascinating.

Videos & DVDs

- The best videos available are short clips on the website of the Monterey Bay Aquarium (www.mbayaq.org). See acorn barnacles filtering, anemones cloning, hermit crabs shoveling it in, and more.
- Video clips on nudibranchs and more available at the National Marine Sanctuaries website: www.oceanservice.noaa.gov

Index

Photographs are numbered in **boldface** and follow the print references after **PP** (photo page).